Pleadings from the Pleiades

Ken Jones

DEDICATION

This book is dedicated to all the contactees, abductees and scanners of the sky who know in their bones

we are not alone. On a more personal note, this text would not exist without my friend and Webmaster

Steve Luksic, who first guided me towards the lights from above.

FORWARD

The genesis of this manuscript emerged from experiences and insights I had while living in Los Angeles, especially, but also confirmed as I traveled to places such as Nevada, Jamaica, and Sedona, Arizona.

I'll leave it to readers to determine their opinion of my veracity and/or sanity. However, I would also ask all who read this book to keep an open mind and at least admit that the path to true wisdom begins by admitting what we don't know.

My thanks first and foremost go to Peggy Zuleika Lynch, the grande dame of the Texas Poetry scene, and the generous support of Poetry in the Arts Publications in making this book possible. In addition, my gratitude goes to my fellow Art Institute instructor Lisa Lott, who typed and edited and otherwise midwifed this final product. And finally, I'd like to acknowledge the ongoing support of my mentor at the Art Institute of Houston, Dr. Ken Pascal. I hope you enjoy the poems that follow.

Ken Jones

Houston TX 9-09

ACKNOWLEDGEMENTS

The following poems have previously appeared in the places listed below. The poet apologies for any errors or omissions.

Pleadings from the Pleiades (Chapbook)

The Apocalypse of Ken

I Am a Diadem

Bowling with Crowley

Bertrand Russell's Favorite Words

Flat on Our Backs, Sedona, Poco Diablo

Why God Drives a Flying Saucer

Roswell

Horse Warrior Chant

Protest

Upstairs in a Guest Room

What Ken Wrote on the Rock at Sedona

The World of Poet Ken (Website)

Diversities Digitize the Divine

Paralyzed in the Wheel Chair

The Keyhole (Art Institute of Houston)

The Lazy Layabout

For the Spirit of the Drum

Wide-Eyed Angels Angle For a New Fangled Time

Lone Stars

Contact

Carpet of Pretense at

Map of Austin Poetry

Contact

Farfelu

In the Interval

Poetry in the Arts

Your Place in the Multiverse

Patchwork Poems

Watch How They Don't Hurt Their Young

EPIGRAPHS

Be patient-watch again another night-the

Pleiades shall emerge,

They are immortal

"On the Beach at Night"

Walt Whitman

In the still of autumn see the Pleiades.

Far out on the sands, danger in the furze.

North of their tents is surely the sky's end

Where the sound of the river streams beyond the border.

—"On the Frontier"

Li Ho (791-817)

*Note: In ancient Chinese cosmology the flickering of the Pleiades was an omen of alien invasion.

Contents

Part I **11**

Contact 12

The Apocalypse of Ken 13

There Ain't Nobody Home 17

I Am a Diadem 18

Spirit Theorem Proofs 19

Who is Adam Kadmon? 20

Bowling with Crowley 21

Bertrand Russell's Favorite Words 22

In the Interval 23

Your Place in the Multiverse 24

The Lazy Layabout 25

Rituals Righting the Wrong 26

Otherwordly Traditional Cultures 27

For L 15* 28

The Time is Now 29

Beverwill Park 30

Flat on Our Backs, Sedona, Poco Diablo 32

Kukaniloho 33

From Misanthrope to Lycanthrope 34

Random Guidance 35

Implementation 36

Great Spirit Between the Bridges 37

Respect 39

Why God Drives a Flying Saucer 40

Part II **43**

The Reality of the Rulers 44

Must We Weed the Yard? 45

Diversities Digitize the Divine 46

What Exists in Leasts 47
Dying Earth and Its Progeny 48
Doomed Cell by Cell 49
Where the Fight Fled 50
A Conspiracy of Spirits 51
Dying Spirit Balls 52
Burrowing into the Aliens 53
For the Spirit of the Drum 54
Zapped to Next Existence 55
The universes in molecules 56
Roswell 57
Marlovian Heresies, Pts. 1-11 58
Horse Warrior Chant 59
Paralyzed in the Wheel Chair 60
Watch How They Don't Hurt Their Young 61
Carpet of Pretense at 62
Xenophobia 63
Terza Rima Firma, Fermi? 64
Protest 65
Upstairs in a Guest Room 66
What Ken Wrote on the Rock at Sedona 67
Wide-Eyed Angels Angle For a New Fangled Time 68
Again and Again, He Ran the Wrong Way 74

Part I

Contact

I take leave of these pages
When my senses have taken flight
The Mothership breaks into stages
Zigzagging "S" movements of light
I take leave of these pages.

My senses have left me believing
Mother Earth's girded by a fleet.
Other creatures currently receiving
Tolerance consciousness like a pet treat
My senses have left me believing

My own eyes saw the stars move
My partner saw it all, as well
We have no way to prove
The truth of what we tell
My own eyes saw the stars move.

My own mind knows some place beyond
This place must exist
Evidence is slim-we live in a pond
Reality smashes with a fist
My own mind knows someplace beyond

My daily bread is humble crumbs
My daily drink a brackish water
While most folks tally money's sums
I hear the birds plan to fly farther
My daily bread is humble crumbs.

The Apocalypse of Ken

For you who do not see the future
Let this eschatology teach.

In the days when the Prophets become a public nuisance
And none will feed nor clothe nor hear them;
Chaos spreads across the land; Great cities lie empty.
Terrible calamities will befall the deafened populace
Mothers and Fathers will slay their sons who utter
God-given messages.

The Heralds of the Last Summons trumpet
To both the reverent and heretic.
Who truly knows the order in the Book of Life?
When the last copy of the Doomesday Book is on CD-ROM
There will I burn the Libraries and you will all fall
Backwards to a foraging mode.

Then Earth Mother shakes awake, overthrows the yoke
Of overgrown human spawn—heed this prophecy!
You who sleep through the end-time
For He says to me—you will be stranded
In a place far worse than your current hell
Where riptides of dung and blood drown
Any crying screed you let loose in your synods of need.

Fourteen men of God turned into
Bloodied half-maked penitents.
Iron-tipped leather whips appear

Mephistopheles' phallus—beating themselves
With Satan's tool brings Spirit closer.

Then the hen, the hen will rise and not be killed in sin
By that, the sanctuary will be cleansed.
You who use pseudonyms shall be smite like Nimrod
Plaster the yeast of the whore of Babylon across your
        fancy faces.

The Flagellant Monks observed, wondering
How and Why? How and Why?—and Lo
There was an answer because while no one
Shall know the day nor hour, verily,
One may see the How and Why.

Before the Western calendar spits forth three zeros again
Men will descend who proclaim, "I am the Holy Spirit."
Spirit will guide some to the Light; others to a dark frenzy.

Heed! This Sybil makes no errors. 3 false prophets
Will rise in 6 months time. Spewing forth the vilest lies
Talking falsely of a heavenly paradise while signing believers
Onto the ledgers of eternal torment.
They will mid-wife an anti-Christ in a stone grotto
Out of the glare of the mass media. In media res.

Then out of the womb of the prophet
(Which shall be his dung yielding nether regions)
This anti-Christ emerges. His single eye the crucible
Through which the power of anti-Light flies.
His teeth, sharp as a thresher's, curve downward.
He'll utter mirthless words with an unperfumed mouth
Yet many will hear manna and follow his foul urgings.

Your lesson in theodicy will be complete
When you grovel before a trickle of fetid water
Grateful for the poison. When you eat dirt and bless
The nourishment of the earthworms. When you shit your piles
On cold tile and break into cold sweats vomit alleviates.
Scarcity. Security. Theodicy. The choice isn't yours.

When this ultimate evil sinks its footholds into all Earth thought
Then will come One who stands against
Who is sent from the sky beings who farm your sphere for food
Who feverently pray this time you will not be led astray
Whose Pleadings from the Pleiades you ignore at your soul's peril
Who have genetically altered your DNA for the triumph
        of Light to come.

The Paraclete in this One will cause breezes to rise
Will send white petals before his path
Will come to embrace, not hate; for you will see his knowledge
By the feathers which appear by his side.

Then by the Lake of Fire, which manifests the wrath and love
The seed beings feel for you, their seedlings,
These two will battle through you, the souls of the living
To see who will rule and who remains in the realm of
        the never dead.

To Ahura Mazda, we bring embryos of those worthy
The humpback lunatics and impotent lepers being of a kind,
                                Children of the Light.
The Mother's breast milk will turn to molten metal
Incapable of succoring the valleys of life
Able to fill the cavities of hell.

We live in Kali cycle—wintry nobility is our banner.
The arrogant, powerful, and pleasurable replace
The learned, virtuous, and productive.
The die is cast. Die, Caste.

You must abandon all privileges of a noble birth on a search for truth
When you find such enlightenment, your time of toil and troubles ends.
The end time begins.

There Ain't Nobody Home

Insistent resistance rises in masses
The low Seer disappears, clear shadow
Blinds battalions of full power.

One in a million reduced to the One
Irreducible essence—its Presence encompasses
The truly unknown Day or Hour.

A reprieve for freedom—even gaffes have to laugh
As the nephew coughs up primogeniture phlegm balls
Catered and masked in the Debutante's crack.

Metastasize a contradicted bleeding lung
Already inside, she's drowning, she's drowning
Insistent resistance to a new low Lawgiver

An insurrection protected rises in the West
Dissect this discussion—sign on the cross
The Saucer fought to fly them here,—now who's home?

I Am a Diadem

I am a sweat drenched dog in the summer heat.
I am a dying soldier lying in a Hummer's seat.
I am love crazed flesh awash in ultraviolet light.
I am a shadow knower turning my face to dark bright.
I am a suicidal dollop of egg and sperm and spirit.
I am a serious argument for term limits.
I am a scarred diatribe of a long worried scribe.
I am a modem once connected to my Father's scrotum.
I am an inexorable evolution in biotechnology.
I am the seed of extraterrestrial animal husbandry.
I describe situations as my tribe bribes me to silence.
I am an exotic example of alien bioscience.
I am a software package for a skywatching hacker.
I am a wheezing paybacker, convulsing with laughter.
I am a solipstic sophist, used to confusing you
I am a troubled team raging with an ambient view
I am a radiant Reality enraptured by an atom's capture
Of an ironic, bionic, myopic sinecure.
Sure, I'm a fool, but ignore at your peril
Sign off tonight, they're shooting fish in a barrel.

Spirit Theorem Proofs

In my utter otherness
I am excluded from connection
Within a small circle:
The Unity of All.

Bursting to explode this quarantine
My moon-dust-contaminated psyche
Likes to flatter itself as a satellite
Whose revolutions truly matter
To the roiling Earth looming in my horizon.

But my tidal triumph inevitably
Lies exhausted on a rocky promontory
Or filthy, plastic-bottle covered beach
In silent shame my utterance
Offers other proofs of nothing.

Who is Adam Kadmon?

The En-Sof is far beyond
Any mind in Man, there, Sun.
So relax, take that burden off your back
Forces of Light remain to attack.

Adam Kadmon on a search of truth
Who is the One of Light, Youth,
Forces the forces of goodness to emerge
After generations of pain and hidden stations
Purged to a corner of a rented house
Adam Kadmon is simply a mouse
Hooked into an Apple Computer
Don't hate him when he shoots her.
Adam Kadmon was the One we yearn
To resurrect, inspect, then burn
Ezekial talked to the sky creatures today
They said, "Don't call us they"

Adam Kadmon is the Man, the Homeboy
That no devil pyramid money can buy
Don't tell me 'bout your numbers, honey,
I'm totally broke, the En-Sof: "Enough!"

Why the Buddhists say "Oh, no!"

Bowling with Crowley

Solar blood streams through my holy form
The amirath plastered across my façade
Yields a demon thought—offers now caught
Where the Cosmic Masters blast disasters
By this apocalypse driven scrivener.

For all we know, we shall return
To this place in the Ayurvedic cycle.
Or trapped like a Jainist infested with mites
We will allow our spirit beliefs to eat us.
To defy the urge to deify hides the why.
So ensconsed in the spiral eye,
A typhoon festooned with Typhoid Mary posters
Postulates a virgin Jesus to altar
Hot atop the Mayan circle toaster.

Bertrand Russell's Favorite Words

Begrimed Pilgrims lost in a subliminal quagmire
Fulminate about the ineluctable apocalypse
Golden wind knocks them back, inspissated.
Alabaster skin turns incarnadine
Chrysoprase glistens, Health's talisman.
In alembic ecstasy, the Spirir drops down
Gaia's terraqueous diapason.

In the Interval

A nearby star, say
21 light years away
Goes nova.
But in the interval
I have "Time" to say
My bedtime prayers
From birth to Earth's
Electromagnetic grave
Then another event occurs.

Your Place in the Multiverse

Proud debauchee, you stand astride a life
Devoted to decadence and pure pleasure.
The measure of your success is the strife
You carry as a sacred treasure.

Yet at the last moment, you try to reach
Some rapproachment with what Spirit's here.
All these wounds have lessons to teach
About facing existence without fear.

Earth rushes through space; we are pinned
Then another universe begins.

The Lazy Layabout

I guess that Keats and Swinburne
And the bards in days of yore
Laid in yards to live and learn
And lazily lay some more.

The life of a poet is a layabout
Barely able to lift a hand
Then suddenly seized to jump and shout
"A vile curse on the homeland!"

Mostly dishonored and ignored voices
Congregate in ghostly choruses
Lamenting their now ineluctable choices
Spirited to confusion by uncontrollable forces

Old enough to know that this is it
Yet still confronted by the pull beyond
The Poet's task: To rise when others sit
To speak of Spirit's mirror in the pond.

Rituals Righting the Wrong

Sun God heat consumption mountain
Over human forms the blood flows warm
Sacrificial children who when asked at seven
Throw themselves on the scythes of heaven
With Incan gold and Mayan maize
Your power and glory fully blaze
On this place lighted from your heights
Let it reign o'er battles, peaceful nights
Vicious temple priests in flight
The last child out must close the door
Not knowing all the whys and wherefores
Meet in his aspect and his eye
So for us all soon here will die.

Quetzal bird! You channel
What? The maize waving tall
In the fields swept clean by breeze?
Or forces beyond the temporal
Tapestries these weave?

Otherwordly Traditional Cultures

Strange bedfellows
A demographic transition
Reason, the agenda
For troubled children

Catalog deterioration
Embrace an explosion
Of senseless well being
All-seeing proposals

Fiddle while the numbers
Play nice sounding anarchy
A plutocratic autarky
Of stark empowerment

Famine and disease arise
As the human family size
Culls the gentle and wise
To join the lights in the skies.

For L 15*

<u>Beware</u>, <u>O</u> <u>Artists</u>! Outsiders or in
The female Kali Yuga awaits your sin.
Agents of Kronos drive you to anger
Beware white light! The danger, the danger!
Golk Golk! The females with the Great O
Deep in your fetid guts you know
Alien pyramids meet the camel's eye
Thog! Thog! Artists! Don't cry!
You will not see alone, I shall be there
Bones and sinews, and you—truth or dare?
If truth, the Kali Yuga awaits with her evil
Beware, Kronos-child, if you fill her full
For she is the white light, the danger, the devil!

*L 15 takes his name from the Intergalactic Angels that visit and converse
with him.

The Time is Now

Portents of Armageddon in the porous sky
Pour on us the wrath of spirits long thought dry
Drown us in another bout of poison air
Who are we? Why are you? You Mean—We're Where?

Helicopter circles over choking oceans
Birds swill a killing brew—a dying potion
Unseen leading forces us to focus on the end
Finale of a used-up planet, damn it: it descends.

This is not the breeze of your unease
This is the harsh wind that does you as it pleases
Hot in its path—a search and rescue squad
Recues your miscues, line up to God

I read in the yellowed leaves of ancient texts
Facts have wrecked our salvation—baby, what's next?

Signs of the divine dying time riddle our fingers
The hot hand of the Lord in these cool breezes lingers
Demons come in over airwaves destined to continue
This is the medium of the message for you and you.

Beverwill Park

I.

I know the celestial acolytes are amidst us always
Debating the Consolidated Truths.
Politics is the balance of competing economic interests.
Direct guidance by random chance.

Why the nerve of the wind, observed again!
Your moccasins firmly tied with One
White Man lace and seagulls chirping.
Politics is the balance of competing Economic interests,

"Sell me something, Mister" says the retarded schoolgirl
Gripping her thighs, you swore you heard her utter
"Syntax is a pound of butter."
Direct guidance by random chance.

II.

The glassy-eyed children shoehorn workers into boxes
Disregarding occasional shamelessness.
My moccasins firmly tied and seagulls chirping
I ran out of interest in my life long ago.

Lady Connecticut Frobisher Dickeragin
Pounded on the veranda like the Lord's chosen.
Sir Mildren Groper <u>con</u> glover
Anamolous in the role of her lover.

Disregarding occasional shamelessness
Sir Edward Lyall keeps the peace
The glassy eyed children shoehorn workers into boxes
"Sell me something, Mister" says the retarded schoolgirl
Politics is the balance of competing Economic interests

III.

"I hate my maid" my nephew says
Right in my uncaring face.
Concrete of the purest whiteness
Or iridescent plastic products sold by the gross
Equally mirrored in my oh-so-special eyes.

After every few disasters, I'm called by the Sky Masters
To Debate the Consolidated Truths.
As I repeatedly bang my helmet-covered head
Against our society wiping away history, I sputter

"Politics is the balance of competing Economic interests!"
I succumb to the dun-colored leather valise
Its false face—a spreadsheet striptease.
"Sell me something, Mister" said the retarded schoolgirl
Overwhelmed in the Lost Angel Hospital.

IV.

So the whole thing strikes you as futile too
Out of control for uncounted millennia
Pronounced failures falter like a foreign tongue
Right in my uncaring face

For Doug Wills

Flat on Our Backs, Sedona, Poco Diablo

As we talked about initial offerings
Corporate holdings and the Republicans
A meteor soared into our atmosphere.

Kukaniloho

See the Pleiades in sacred November
Holy red stones fire at sunrise
Another aili'i awaits to stir
First opening of tiny eyes

Fourteen chiefs surround the mother
Witnessing this royal birth
Testifying to unseen forces
Of this whelp's station and worth

At the mountainous navel of Oahu
Twenty one more High Chiefs and Lords
Watch one wield a blade of bamboo
Severing the newborn's umbilical cord

Soon the solstice will guide the high men
Through the cycle of time and back again
Another young mother is brought here in pain
Another noble child descends and ascends

After hundreds of years of enforced quiescence
Sacred circle and I commune in silence
Brought here somehow by divine guidance
The ancients animate aili'i defiance

From Misanthrope to Lycanthrope

Seriously caring would involve staring beyond the sun to the multiple universes waiting in your blindness. Milton's kindness extends to oedipal bends – heretic callisthenic lens. Glaucoma sufferer or hippie puffer – see green as alien ween – white foam – Gray come – Nordics sick on driftwood straws and shells. Is purgatory nugatory? Thank God the Nazi Pope dropped "Prince of the West" as well as hell of unbaptized children. Nigerian primates hate liberation theology. Afghan courts berate apostates. Fundamentalists LDS ride child brides. Monotheism's backward tribal jism spewed by Zeta Reticuli controllers whose Motherships gird our globe. Watching as their anal probe – the lax laxative – releases a cloaca of catastrophes when we need a tipping point palliative.

Random Guidance

There's a secret alien project on Earth
Convert these species' hate to love at birth
Throw them into environments
In the name of alien bioscience
See if they survive every test of the tribe.

A hopeful life squeeze in the breeze
A blatant spiritual process for a place under siege

Implementation

Its written (now computerized)
Records of the State of the Natural World
Provide Scientists with a basis for understanding
Changes in our Earth's Environment.

The project continues. Kinds and numbers of organisms
Found at a distance on either side of the lines
Furnish priceless information
Managed to withstand increasing tourism.

Regeneration in areas where ill-advised
Reuses to understand the dynamics.
In tropical countries and land management districts
The land is returning to the forests.

Importance is immeasurable.
Yet, few, if any, conduct
These experiments of sponsored priorities
Subject to those who implement them

Great Spirit Between the Bridges

You have steered my course.

In my ignorance, I acknowledged
Only the despair of unknowing.
From my youth, your path
Has shone before me unawares.
My footfalls all lead to a purpose
Which now revealed, repeals
My doubts and peals the bells
Of angels in an all filled light.

Why have I been Chosen
For this place and this time. My message
Is the eternal One heard again.
You have told me there will be many unbelievers
Those who will not listen.

Still, I have a hard time understanding why
In the land of the Lost Angels
You have proved you heard my prayers.

We do not like arrogance
The Creatures of Light told me.

They came to me in tangible form
Said, "They're the only two of their kind left."
Then I broke down and cried
While the eternal footman scraped his heel
I could only feel remorse

Regret at my ignorant denial
Denial of my ignorance and regret.

The Universal Love sees all, knows ALL
The sure mercies of humble holiness
Between the bridges—know the Spirit.

Respect

Stuck inside a small town
Also a tired mind
My body, weak as All Get Out
Wonder what the future finds?

One World vision here today
On Venice Beach, what I say
Occurs before by very eyes
We share a world under blue skies

A Tower of Babel we embrace
Life—it was the Janus face
Each side a desperate façade
If my name was Mod Squad

And now the birds fly up above
Dirty, clean,—eternal Love
What of it, don't you understand?
Does it matter what Brand

Is burned into my red hot arm?
An Injun knows the good of harm
When your kind thought I'd bought the farm
I really stood, deadly, unarmed

Owning nothing but a view of everything
As all connected wonder—she brings
This goddess planet with which we're blessed
We live to give in Spirit—Respect.

Why God Drives a Flying Saucer

"You, like your world, are selfish; not I—
I gamble everything to be what I am"—Julia De Burgos

I.
In the old part of the city
She departs to disagree.
Lucky in what you know,
All apoplectic,
In the shadow of the window,
Reflections in triplicate
Stumble secretly over my predicate.
I subjugate her subject for a reason.

This in-season treason
Is a solitary confinement. Your souls lost
Refinement lays wreaths at your door.

Borne back by a desperate suture
Your pure pose melts in this resolve:
    I have no purpose; I have no proof
    I have no sight to see except what's truth
    I have no scepter; apparition at the ridge
    I have no way to take away this edge.

II.
Waves wash sharply over our poses.
In a crimson and gold party,
we enjoy these patriots.
Hagiography clings to cotton

Troublesome Maos invade by video.
Depleted middles fall empty, collapse
Into a closure, cornered in a synapse
Haymakers in hyperspace go:
"Why? Where? Four!"
Of us suspended
If not upended.

III.
Perhaps this will fill
The in and out of focus days
Unfazed in mazes, you say
"Hocus Pocus!" Still more
Understanding hands perused
Sharp in some weird, wired angle
The key chrome dangles
Lost in the editing bay.
Perhaps this will fall
In and out of focus or
Amaze in stages
You might say "Hocus Pocus"

Special effects are helpless here.
Nuclear waste in hasty fears;
Canceled checks, and all that
That implies the universal why
That implies the universal why.

Once I lived for
I now know only to die
What I before believed
I now see to be a lie.

IV.
In the electricity, a secret whispers
Lit through the power grid
We don't know when to quit.
Some sad fantasy
Plays itself in your reality.

We, the wild young men of Paradigm
We have come for your children
Because God Drives a Flying Saucer
With almond eyes and probing tongue

Jesus navigates the alien craft.
Electricity flows through us
Eternity—my Maker's Mark
Discern in me an undying spark
Beyond the horror of the dark
Cosmos flow so real
That energy is the one consistency
Of a schoolish, standoffish design.

V.
My eyes are blanks. My words, shells.
Loaded to blow us straight to hell.
Traps sprung, at the top of your lungs
She screams flat on her back, skull cracks
Bleed out her belly like holiday turkey—
Sure, surely, here, truly,
The murky work is you and me.

Part II

The Reality of the Rulers

These souls have come out of the imperishable light
With the spirit of truth within them.
All who know this way live deathless in the midst
Of a dying planet, a dissipating polity.
They shall refuse to enter marriage, business
Or any webs of this world.
They are an undominated generation
Pledged to Great Spirit's return.

Since you asked about the existence of the cosmic rulers
I will tell you they are real.
They fly through eyes of light
Illuminated souls, and whatever other devices
They use to reuse your spirit.
A lone Indian woman singing upon a barren plain
A neon display disparaging suicide and hubris
Television scientist's overprecise numerology
Disembodied voices describing earthly princes
As if they were nothing but experimental animals
For the rulers of the universe and forces of evil
For those who sin against the whole
Shall find the light entire has taken their vision.

Must We Weed the Yard?

The cotton pollen of a weed
Whips its whisps in the wind
Seed survivor of a near freeze
Life sap surges in your stems.
Why should I have to kill you
Rip your life out at the root
Just because you dared to appear?
Here in silence crested Suburbia
We can't have evidence of wildness.
Appearances are all; facades are everything.
What if the fat-cheeked stockbroker
And his mottle-thighed wife
Wander through, intent to buy, then spy
Your confused diffuseness around the lawn?
Surely they'll flee in fear
No lovers of the clover here!

We each seek a home somewhere amongst the Earth,
You in your leafy variety feed off sun and dirt.
I, in my decadent appurtances, live off Society's shards.
The stockbroker and his wife, desiring pristine yards
Swap numbers and paper to slake their hungers.
If some celestial congregation bolted in from the Blue
Sky wide above and thundered about our Oneness who
Would truly listen or, if hearing, understand
And act to keep the Life amidst this land?

Diversities Digitize the Divine

We all believe our stigmata are unique.
On the Cyberspace Scriptorium
Monks preserve monkey knowledge.
The reality of prayer
Transmogrified into a terminal
Access to the Nexus
At once trapped in a spot
Yet everywhere and nowhere.

During the Grand Silence
I hear a clicking of keys
Unlocking hidden universes
Diverse as we please.
On their knees, Diversities
Digitize the divine
A sign of recurring excrescenses
Dense as existence.

Your bloody sweat fools no one
Into knowing nothing is something.
Prophetic communications abate
When Dog Orgies dissipate.
For two to three days, wounds in your forehead
Are signs of unused force.
They do not invade. Listen
To what they say before it's too late.

What Exists in Leasts

Gaia abounds
In all forms around

Dying Earth and Its Progeny

Wheezing amidst the cheese and sleaze
A gray, blasé breeze
Cloaks and chokes manhandled land—
Nirvana from afar on its face is Inferno.
Valhalla where past shackles dissolve
Into soulless self-interest hovels
Freedoms portioned into tiny parcels
A polyglot merchant mélange—
These tribes might survive
By amending past procedures
Where intra-species contact yielded
Hatred, claustrophobic, xenophobic—
But hopes are low.
From a genetic mix theoretically
A mindless best ensues.

Doomed Cell by Cell

On a flat asphalt plane
One thousands cars a minute
Deludedly view as urbane
Selves shackled by dirt and soot
A lone man stands
In dirt piles where his feces lands
Foul air drives his palsy cough
No better off, no better off.
Both tribes hardened by it all to fear
Next scene's sun turn
Moon glow and burn
And both yearn
Doomed never to learn
The dirt, the grime
And erosions of time are their bride.
Both seek warm dry hives to hide
And answer Nature's gut and gonad hungers.
Till the dreary daily dying cell by cell takes its toll
They stand and praise these fields they graze
As both heaven and hell.

Where the Fight Fled

A million reactions
Dissections and dissensions
Rendering rancor—
The Random's anchor.
I a rogue electron
On an isolated isotope
Careening between orbits
In hubristic hope
Six billion primates
Whose birthright hate
Settles like silt in
Their unsettled state
Can resplatter the pattern
Of resources divorced
From holistic need
To feed naked greed
To a semblance of sense and equivalence
But a million reactions
Dissections and dissensions
Can only render
My surrender.

A Conspiracy of Spirits

Inside a downtown
Hordes of lawyers contemplate
How Capital can next build cities—
What power plants in which states
Will feel the colossal why
Of lonely terrified primates
Puffed with pride into human form
Become the bum and the heir.

In the exhaust thickened air
I hear the screeches of wreaking cars
Barred by inertia from evaporating into circuses.

This evil inside this building
Cannot kill the pulsating Spirit of the Land
Though its hollow paper shallowness
Tries mightily to dull the Spirit
of the Trees which made the paper.

A Conspiracy of Spirits
Unseen in the tightly controlled climate
Waits to rise, is rising, will rise to sting
their dull unfeeling eyes.

Dying Spirit Balls

OUT, damned lies, You don't own my Spirit
It breathes in corn fields, moved ion wind
Rewinds to a peaceful place
Graces all amazing places across from us

Do you feel the grass on your face?
The breeze from a distant place
The Earth, she answers back
Life Spirit on the attack—bring it back
Bring it back?

An unconscious notion something's wrong
You try to escape—to sin a ton
Now atone, atone for lost truth
Costs you pay to uncover why

Get back in there and do Your job!
Forces of the devil's evil call.
You will not sign onto his list
You will not need him if you resist
Until your dying spirit balls itself into a fist
To pound upon the table—no
more! nomore!
I'm alive, I hear—what is
<u>is</u> the score
Sewer disk reflect the sun
Now get back on the run
and tell the story
It's only scary if you let it be.

Burrowing into the Aliens

The alien controller bitch bled all over my tongue. My gums
congealed into universal stew and the livers fed overmuch
Into the gnarly gulch.

Which style beguiles you now? Putrid piles, diamond bile, all
the while, the Cantankerous cancer victim chick throws her bald
head into the sick pit. Gross as it is, it is not the sickest
lickety split ever under the torn asunder hell-sky.

Fire here all the time. Cold on some levels, on others just
too warm. Harm me again, God above. Your love is in the One
in the homeless bum. On the regal front, the shattered interiors.
Fear not this shot into void. Alloyed senses defend insenseless.

The Alien controller folded the bad old bitch in the teeth.
Rotten and rotting, the finger pointed at Uranus. From all around
the orbital path, the wrath of oxygen wrung down a curtain of
burn.
The nitrogen hypered to another data set; the hydrogen com-
pressed
into a Hydrox cookie. Nookie waited to eat and ooze its soothing
wet chute on your best boot. Loot my love; cute to this glowing
lute you say "Cuz, she's for you"—but her mind unwinds like
a toy soldiers. you hold her and say, "Alien, mail in this
masturbatory rebate, please."

For the Spirit of the Drum

Young reader, whose burnished hungers
The world waits next to turn away,
Let the undulating sea's spirit-catching waves
Show the way to a higher frequency further in the future.
An open spot known only by those whose
Present position importunes a portable essence
Retrieved from the gulls cries in the high sun sky
Which in wintry will find the why in its way.

Young spirit, remember your soul cannot continue
If you abandon the chain of life
Absent yourself from the names reified
In your reproduction function deified.
The Sky-Masters stay Light while you
Born of woman and man return to a flesh-dessicated state
Finger food for systolic moods
Measure the pressure by one gesture:
Listen and let in who moved this wanderer to perform
This act willed into life for both sharer and creator.

Young hopeful one, go into your tasks with respect
For the spirit of the drum which calls again
To unite all forces of Earth, sea, sky,
For the life behind the not hollow but purposeful
Sound abandoning, rebounding, surrounding
Showing a glow. For all who see will now
Know the message sung by the Light left in your eye.

Zapped to Next Existence

When the celestial chorus called
Guiding me to switch universes
Created beings, jostling endlessly
Spun my spirit like a mouseball

Unwilling to log off the physical
I demanded defenestration
Landing in my current incarnation
At the windowsill of the material
The Universes in Molecules

The ice slaps back an air bubble
The coals respond in time
The computer started bleeping
The poet tried to rhyme

The universes in molecules

Raged at ancient fates
This realm, hardly at the helm
Dispenses with debate

Here and now allows somehow
The All where we are stalled
This place is a precious kiss
But next moment, we are called

To give back to the shocking crack
Of galaxies in our sizzling trees
Frosty Earth is melting, falling,
Bringing the rock apes to their knees

And we aliens are pleased.

Roswell

Roswell, Roswell
Place where their spirits dwell
Illuminated for the chosen few
How about you?
You must listen when the time comes
Hear Earth dying, then hear their hum
Many are called, but few know
Who will tell the people?
Who will tell the people?
Here's the energy.
Now?

Marlovian Heresies, Pts. 1-11

Are you willing not to be afeard of bugbears and hobgoblins?
Holy Communion would be better administered as a bong hit.
St. John the Evangelist was bedfellows with Christ and used him
as the sinners of Sodom do
Until he comes in you.

Oh, to domineer in taverns, scaring multitudes of plain folks
Neither Goodman Satan, not Sir Reverence, nor Beelzebub's Butt
Plug
Every say, "Come. I think Hell's a fable."
A stanza declarative after an envoy is like a fart before a good
stool.
The House of Mine Enemies has for its coat of arms three dog
turds reeking
A foot-taker for coach horses—an oratorical yokel of vainglory.
The gravediggers were busy this plague summer
This tasteless bagatelle—not for my spirit this season.

Look what a hook the Lord put in the nostrils of this barking dog
Speed freak geeks, weaker than weak, don't deserve to speak

In my own hand, I wrote blasphemies
Like an epicure and atheist, seeking a pitiful end.
Will I even curse to my last gasp?
Together with my breath an oath flew out my mouth.
A gentleman and property owner who served like a rent-boy.

Horse Warrior Chant

I hear the horses of the warriors
Callously slaughtered by my ancestors
I am here to return the favor
To Earth and her cosmic masters.
Spirit—shake this place awake
Take this plane by the scruff of the neck
Then break its ungodly evil back
To return it to the Light right on track.

I am the horse beneath the feet
Of a Great Spirit whose defeat
Then resurrection has begun preordained
Cleanse our goddess of the reckless human stain
Then let it transmogrify into a manifest why
Surround the turbulence with a single eye
In the center, a vortex to wreck
The vestigial anti-spiritual speck.

Paralyzed in the Wheel Chair

Male murderers try to stifle Mother Earth's oracles
But the prophetess' glossolalia flows like a miracle

The prophetess chews laurel leaves
As she comes all over me
Then she drinks bulls' balls blood
In the beeswax temple. She slips fern seeds
Into her sacral vessel
The supplicants' honey-cakes overflow.

She feeds on sacred flesh
A ram prepared in sacrifice
The songbirds on the golden roof
Dive like divining dice
A copper coin upon the eyes
A secret well by an old oak tree.
Can you see the future, sister?
Will you share this Earth with me?
Remember to forget Memory
To pray to the Moon for Good Fortune
And answer prayers in dreams
And bathe in the path of the deities.

Watch How They Don't Hurt Their Young

Tap the tip of the cup
Your living wind, your loving waters
Your shining light
At the end of a long night
Of frightening, frantic running
Both toward and away from you
I sought you in every corner
Of my decadent life.
My strife the hidden pain
At finding you, yet refusing
To admit defeat.
And in your victory
You showed me
How the triumph was all of ours.
Mine, if only I dared
To carry the banner.
Theirs, by their very being.
Your seed lies deeply in the Spirits,
I listen to its first root
Break the husk.

Carpet of Pretense at

What we purloined
What we purchased
Floods in our veins
Carpet of Deity breath

What we encapsulate
What we emasculate
Switch to the next station
Pretense all emaciated

What we dissected
Weren't nothin'—dessicated
Morph in shadow's fire
Dormant with the cormorants.

Xenophobia

A common enough condition
To fix before the invasion

They are not marauders
We must change our mindset
That condemns outsiders as barbarians
Judges others' odd habits

Or adaptations, more accurately,
To whatever need fulfillment presented
Reduced to a moral de minimus
We devolve without cause or animus

Avoid harming others—except for sustenance
If then, minimize the suffering
These tenets can grow you from a tiny Buddah
To a mid-sized Siddhartha

Terza Rima Firma, Fermi?

Above the alien moon, warmed by harm
Below the target of a turret, glow
Princes enwrapped in numismatic gloves.

Flase waltz steps to the fore on the floor
Chateaus of pure expression abound
Without fail; Landscapes chuckle humbly.

Harmonious chords implore; no less, no more
Prime oppression lies like poison on the land
Bucks chuckle, locked in behind, below.

Twist as the Joust, assessed a technical
Redeems the seemingly pointless pointillist's kiss
Miss this. Listen to the new phrase's phase.

Protest

Poets are not <u>against</u> the universe
Knowing that humans are not more than rocks
Nor that rocks dominate our fate.
But that each instant of honest existence
Makes poets out of rocks
And atoms into poets.

Upstairs in a Guest Room

Upstairs in a guest room
The pure products of Corporate America <u>are</u> crazy.
Suicide by monoxide? Why not
Douse myself in gasoline then drink a tumbler
Or slam a shot before I light my fire?
I could never fill up my tank
At the neon oasis where All bought on credit
Tends to blend into nothing, anyway.
Afford me this opportunity to utter this anti Babbit babble
Before I bend again, a lying whore
To the Almighty devil Dollar.
Hollering, I strike a match
Together, we dispatch
This business for the Day.

What Ken Wrote on the Rock at Sedona

Great Spirit—
Come back.

Wide-Eyed Angels Angle For a New Fangled Time

I.
Up above, an alien controller waits—blinking
Lost —thinking
Found in space
An alien controller finds a face
Who fled the battlefield,
If not for the fight he might have said
Nothing's worth knowing tonight.

All lost in Great Spirit's path.
Are we among the last like that?
We cannot disagree
We must save it ALL to let what must be be

As we jockey for position
Will either of us listen
To Nature's wavelength?
Let it bring us strength
Know the radio we each tune.
Fandango by the full moon.

The One True God commands me
The One True Way demands me
To lead a spiritual purge
To seek a heart-filled urge
To lead a cosmic surge
To shake awake this place
With a gossamer diadem.

The One True Light assures me
The One True Path will cure me
If I become what's within me
To let it happen effortlessly
To finally fully free me

II.
Talking prophetic fish fly backwards
Words you heard herd hurt
Into piles while the stylish
Offer to buffer
The battle in utter hunger
The alien stifles a laugh
Wondering if it's worth it.

If you think you're beyond good and evil
You won the battle but lost the war
Face the Oneness, trust in us
You are nebulae dust, near and far.
If you think there are no morals
You tossed the truth on a trash pile

Face the goodness, what must shout
Conquer the fear of a full worthwhile.

In the middle of the valley, a house full of bones
The words of the Lord in new neon stones
They came to me and commanded my prophecy
Cancelled all hope but let Now be
The spirits still flow in this place you gave
I live here, their servant, to open the grave
Where they place my Spirit upon my hand
A writing stick's made me sick, I understand.

III.
Hyperspace cybernauts fought
Morphing crimson saucers
Through digital operating revolutions
Systems overwhelmed by viral lights
Crash in bulk, disk space empty.
Black holes in the vortex orbit
Compuserve Duke of knowledge
Bit head lasers incontinent
Osiris, the Goddess, prodigy
Of Prophecy in adobe voyages to the center
Hubris smeared by High 8 Alphas on Betacam
The key to the Information Superhighway
Principia Mathmatica vs. pixel sticks
Indeterminate resonance
Streaming technology from main frames
Networks RAM, Powerbooks shook
By alien downlinks downloaded

disguised as a crash
Through digital operating revolutions
Hyperspace cybernauts fought
Systems overwhelmed by pixel lights
Black holes in the vortex orbit

Bit head prodigies prophecy voyages
Indeterminate resonance, GODDESS knowledge
Network downlink, amped on the offramp
Of the computer supra-freeway
Empty disk space crashes and burns
Morphing crimson saucers

IV.
In the megacities, the sickened air
Makes eminently clear
When Spirit's near
You let it lead or you burn
If you get too close
And know it's noose
You'll be crazy amid

the usual diurnal madness
Born here together upon a lightening wind
We offer thanks for the frightening.
Body and soul—rank 1 & 2
And Spirit makes three
Read tarot cards in the master's why
And be plastered by new anyeurisms
Sworded by knew anyeurisms.

Your Grace, your face
Is the perfect spirit within.
You cannot call this sin

Hurt birds sit placidly by
Winter sun shivers like glitter off the water
A commercial jetliner rises into brown sky
Anima mundi—Logos Spermatokoi
Fill in outhouses
What did you buy yesterday?

More "E", Please. More "E" Please
A thirsty pliant pleads
The Pleiadies remain named
By those not of its worlds

"We used to call them cities"
Says the black girl tyke on a trike
She hates me, so fillets me
To the core of my why
"Tonight we're serving Roman"
Say the body transposing Aliens
Who protect me from flying soccer balls
Then point a door to survival

Then they appear on my TV set
CBS microphones on NBC channel
The spotlight on a white shirted dot
I realize is me—then they have me run crazy
Back and forth like Wrong Way Reigels
Never to find the end zone
Please, Please, don't feed on me
I'll do what you say, what you put me here for
Just keep open a door
To survival, revival, a convivial alien stew
Made out of not me nor you.

V.
Through the burning forest
Happy campers hung around hampering
Relief efforts.
Angels through the Great Cities
Force Man now to understand
Angels fill my confidence, force & peace
Their whip brands flagellated Po Valley slaves
Through the searing hills
Hawks cackle fulfilled.

VI.
Behold the moon's power at mid-day
Enough to wrench unison cackles
From the throat of the flock
Enough to cause One to take wing towards its origin
Enough to whip the wind about my stark lair
Enough to cause this pen to take flight in my hand?

I go to a place of my choosing
To lay on a spot of my choosing
You will, by listening, be choosing

You might choose to truly listen
Or in your choosing, disregard,
Whether the weather affects the hearing
Or the choices we discard.

I will disregard the reasons for choosing
And you, the ocean, will answer,
Slapping against the concrete wall
Then retreating, by your choosing
Hearing only the ALL in the places we are.

VII.
After 2000 years, a longing fills your heart
A bell tingles in Corpus Christi
Two bells toll—the animus mundi
Shakes awake the barren consciousness of ages
Here is the longing of the centuries.

Again and Again, He Ran the Wrong Way

I know you are busy with the day to day worries
Of your life—but I just had to write
Because I had the time. I dropped out
Of the main current of society a while ago.
Now I'm penniless, homeless, but I have the time
To keep in touch, to drop a note to ask how
You are holding up in the face of the craziness out there.
You might write back to tell me you envy
The unstructured pattern I've been planning
Since I sat in my childhood room while my family
Fought like enraged tribes over my brother's problems.
But being ignored helped these words come naturally
So I can only count myself lucky.
Grateful that I have this ancient sanctuary
To return to when my sanity collapsed.
Not to burden you, but that steely strength in my eyes,
That ox-like stride and overstuffed self-confidence
Came tumbling down like dirt from a dump truck
One day last May, or maybe early June
When space aliens came through my television
Pretending to be football announcers shining a spotlight
On one player in an untucked white buttondown, in 3 point stance
Who never quite reached the end zone. Again and again
He ran the wrong way while they watched and laughed.
That was me, I guess you guessed,
And as I reached to pet my cat
Horrible sentences, instructions for her dismemberment,
Appeared in my open copy of the Los Angeles Times.
Then a motherly voice resonated through my head

Saying, "We'd never leave you this way."
But I'd already left myself those years ago
When I sat alone in my room
Pretending what was happening wasn't happening.
I'm telling you all this now because no one
Really likes hearing about my last trip upstate
Or where the next dollar comes from
Or how I lay about and hate the bum I've become.